Video Game Retail Opening & Closing Procedures

A workbook for opening and closing a video game retail store.

Aaron T. Castle

Copyrighted Material

Copyright © 2016 by Aaron T. Castle. All rights reserved worldwide.

No part of this publication may be replicated, redistributed, or given away in any form without the prior written consent of the author/publisher or the terms relayed to you herein.

This workbook may be used to chronicle the everyday opening and closing procedures of a video game retail store for exactly 31 days. The process of such a day-to-day act can be simplified with a simple checklist, so that you as a manager will never forget a step.

Please note that each page of this workbook comes with an opening and closing page back-to-back so that each full day of business is on each page. Complete with sections to record the date and any miscellaneous events not covered in the book.

Opening Procedure

Date _____

- ☐ Arrive at least 30 minutes before opening
- ☐ If there is any signs of forced entry, do not enter and call the police
- ☐ Never open store alone, two or more employees must be present with you
- ☐ Relock door after entering. Let employees in as they arrive
- ☐ Make a visual check of entire store to make sure nothing is out of place and everything looks clean
- ☐ Disable alarms
- ☐ Open safe, remove cash register tills, and set up cash registers
- ☐ Turn on computers at the front desk and make sure they're working properly
- ☐ Check e-mails and respond if needed
- ☐ Turn on display televisions and make sure the advertisements are properly broadcasting on loop
- ☐ Turn on game consoles and make sure they're working properly
- ☐ Organize displays in windows or around store floor
- ☐ Turn on AC/heater, adjust thermostat if needed
- ☐ Start daily task list
- ☐ Schedule lunch and breaks
- ☐ _____
- ☐ _____
- ☐ _____

Closing Procedure

Date _____

- ☐ Turn off any lights after all customers exit the building
- ☐ Turn off front lights
- ☐ Never leave store alone, always exit facility in pairs
- ☐ Place closed sign at window in plain sight
- ☐ Assign closing and cleaning duties to employees
- ☐ Make sure all bathrooms, shelves and floors are completely cleaned
- ☐ Return all refunded items behind front desk or in back room
- ☐ Return any refunded defected items to back room for processing
- ☐ Close out registers, make sure all funds are accounted for
- ☐ Settle credit card machines
- ☐ Generate a detailed batch listing
- ☐ Transmit batch
- ☐ Store all tills in safe and lock it
- ☐ Turn off AC/heat, computers, televisions and game consoles.
- ☐ Lock all necessary perimeter doors
- ☐ Set alarm and exit building
- ☐ _____
- ☐ _____
- ☐ _____

Opening Procedure

Date _____

- ☐ Arrive at least 30 minutes before opening
- ☐ If there is any signs of forced entry, do not enter and call the police
- ☐ Never open store alone, two or more employees must be present with you
- ☐ Relock door after entering. Let employees in as they arrive
- ☐ Make a visual check of entire store to make sure nothing is out of place and everything looks clean
- ☐ Disable alarms
- ☐ Open safe, remove cash register tills, and set up cash registers
- ☐ Turn on computers at the front desk and make sure they're working properly
- ☐ Check e-mails and respond if needed
- ☐ Turn on display televisions and make sure the advertisements are properly broadcasting on loop
- ☐ Turn on game consoles and make sure they're working properly
- ☐ Organize displays in windows or around store floor
- ☐ Turn on AC/heater, adjust thermostat if needed
- ☐ Start daily task list
- ☐ Schedule lunch and breaks
- ☐ _____
- ☐ _____
- ☐ _____

Closing Procedure

Date _____

- ☐ Turn off any lights after all customers exit the building
- ☐ Turn off front lights
- ☐ Never leave store alone, always exit facility in pairs
- ☐ Place closed sign at window in plain sight
- ☐ Assign closing and cleaning duties to employees
- ☐ Make sure all bathrooms, shelves and floors are completely cleaned
- ☐ Return all refunded items behind front desk or in back room
- ☐ Return any refunded defected items to back room for processing
- ☐ Close out registers, make sure all funds are accounted for
- ☐ Settle credit card machines
- ☐ Generate a detailed batch listing
- ☐ Transmit batch
- ☐ Store all tills in safe and lock it
- ☐ Turn off AC/heat, computers, televisions and game consoles.
- ☐ Lock all necessary perimeter doors
- ☐ Set alarm and exit building
- ☐ _____
- ☐ _____
- ☐ _____

Opening Procedure

Date _____

- ☐ Arrive at least 30 minutes before opening
- ☐ If there is any signs of forced entry, do not enter and call the police
- ☐ Never open store alone, two or more employees must be present with you
- ☐ Relock door after entering. Let employees in as they arrive
- ☐ Make a visual check of entire store to make sure nothing is out of place and everything looks clean
- ☐ Disable alarms
- ☐ Open safe, remove cash register tills, and set up cash registers
- ☐ Turn on computers at the front desk and make sure they're working properly
- ☐ Check e-mails and respond if needed
- ☐ Turn on display televisions and make sure the advertisements are properly broadcasting on loop
- ☐ Turn on game consoles and make sure they're working properly
- ☐ Organize displays in windows or around store floor
- ☐ Turn on AC/heater, adjust thermostat if needed
- ☐ Start daily task list
- ☐ Schedule lunch and breaks
- ☐ _____
- ☐ _____
- ☐ _____

Closing Procedure

Date _____

- ❏ Turn off any lights after all customers exit the building
- ❏ Turn off front lights
- ❏ Never leave store alone, always exit facility in pairs
- ❏ Place closed sign at window in plain sight
- ❏ Assign closing and cleaning duties to employees
- ❏ Make sure all bathrooms, shelves and floors are completely cleaned
- ❏ Return all refunded items behind front desk or in back room
- ❏ Return any refunded defected items to back room for processing
- ❏ Close out registers, make sure all funds are accounted for
- ❏ Settle credit card machines
- ❏ Generate a detailed batch listing
- ❏ Transmit batch
- ❏ Store all tills in safe and lock it
- ❏ Turn off AC/heat, computers, televisions and game consoles.
- ❏ Lock all necessary perimeter doors
- ❏ Set alarm and exit building
- ❏ _____
- ❏ _____
- ❏ _____

Opening Procedure

Date _____

- ☐ Arrive at least 30 minutes before opening
- ☐ If there is any signs of forced entry, do not enter and call the police
- ☐ Never open store alone, two or more employees must be present with you
- ☐ Relock door after entering. Let employees in as they arrive
- ☐ Make a visual check of entire store to make sure nothing is out of place and everything looks clean
- ☐ Disable alarms
- ☐ Open safe, remove cash register tills, and set up cash registers
- ☐ Turn on computers at the front desk and make sure they're working properly
- ☐ Check e-mails and respond if needed
- ☐ Turn on display televisions and make sure the advertisements are properly broadcasting on loop
- ☐ Turn on game consoles and make sure they're working properly
- ☐ Organize displays in windows or around store floor
- ☐ Turn on AC/heater, adjust thermostat if needed
- ☐ Start daily task list
- ☐ Schedule lunch and breaks
- ☐ _____
- ☐ _____
- ☐ _____

Closing Procedure

Date _____

- ☐ Turn off any lights after all customers exit the building
- ☐ Turn off front lights
- ☐ Never leave store alone, always exit facility in pairs
- ☐ Place closed sign at window in plain sight
- ☐ Assign closing and cleaning duties to employees
- ☐ Make sure all bathrooms, shelves and floors are completely cleaned
- ☐ Return all refunded items behind front desk or in back room
- ☐ Return any refunded defected items to back room for processing
- ☐ Close out registers, make sure all funds are accounted for
- ☐ Settle credit card machines
- ☐ Generate a detailed batch listing
- ☐ Transmit batch
- ☐ Store all tills in safe and lock it
- ☐ Turn off AC/heat, computers, televisions and game consoles.
- ☐ Lock all necessary perimeter doors
- ☐ Set alarm and exit building
- ☐ _____
- ☐ _____
- ☐ _____

Opening Procedure

Date _____

- ☐ Arrive at least 30 minutes before opening
- ☐ If there is any signs of forced entry, do not enter and call the police
- ☐ Never open store alone, two or more employees must be present with you
- ☐ Relock door after entering. Let employees in as they arrive
- ☐ Make a visual check of entire store to make sure nothing is out of place and everything looks clean
- ☐ Disable alarms
- ☐ Open safe, remove cash register tills, and set up cash registers
- ☐ Turn on computers at the front desk and make sure they're working properly
- ☐ Check e-mails and respond if needed
- ☐ Turn on display televisions and make sure the advertisements are properly broadcasting on loop
- ☐ Turn on game consoles and make sure they're working properly
- ☐ Organize displays in windows or around store floor
- ☐ Turn on AC/heater, adjust thermostat if needed
- ☐ Start daily task list
- ☐ Schedule lunch and breaks
- ☐ _____
- ☐ _____
- ☐ _____

Closing Procedure

Date _____

- ☐ Turn off any lights after all customers exit the building
- ☐ Turn off front lights
- ☐ Never leave store alone, always exit facility in pairs
- ☐ Place closed sign at window in plain sight
- ☐ Assign closing and cleaning duties to employees
- ☐ Make sure all bathrooms, shelves and floors are completely cleaned
- ☐ Return all refunded items behind front desk or in back room
- ☐ Return any refunded defected items to back room for processing
- ☐ Close out registers, make sure all funds are accounted for
- ☐ Settle credit card machines
- ☐ Generate a detailed batch listing
- ☐ Transmit batch
- ☐ Store all tills in safe and lock it
- ☐ Turn off AC/heat, computers, televisions and game consoles.
- ☐ Lock all necessary perimeter doors
- ☐ Set alarm and exit building
- ☐ _____
- ☐ _____
- ☐ _____

Opening Procedure

Date _____

- ☐ Arrive at least 30 minutes before opening
- ☐ If there is any signs of forced entry, do not enter and call the police
- ☐ Never open store alone, two or more employees must be present with you
- ☐ Relock door after entering. Let employees in as they arrive
- ☐ Make a visual check of entire store to make sure nothing is out of place and everything looks clean
- ☐ Disable alarms
- ☐ Open safe, remove cash register tills, and set up cash registers
- ☐ Turn on computers at the front desk and make sure they're working properly
- ☐ Check e-mails and respond if needed
- ☐ Turn on display televisions and make sure the advertisements are properly broadcasting on loop
- ☐ Turn on game consoles and make sure they're working properly
- ☐ Organize displays in windows or around store floor
- ☐ Turn on AC/heater, adjust thermostat if needed
- ☐ Start daily task list
- ☐ Schedule lunch and breaks
- ☐ _____
- ☐ _____
- ☐ _____

Closing Procedure

Date _____

- ☐ Turn off any lights after all customers exit the building
- ☐ Turn off front lights
- ☐ Never leave store alone, always exit facility in pairs
- ☐ Place closed sign at window in plain sight
- ☐ Assign closing and cleaning duties to employees
- ☐ Make sure all bathrooms, shelves and floors are completely cleaned
- ☐ Return all refunded items behind front desk or in back room
- ☐ Return any refunded defected items to back room for processing
- ☐ Close out registers, make sure all funds are accounted for
- ☐ Settle credit card machines
- ☐ Generate a detailed batch listing
- ☐ Transmit batch
- ☐ Store all tills in safe and lock it
- ☐ Turn off AC/heat, computers, televisions and game consoles.
- ☐ Lock all necessary perimeter doors
- ☐ Set alarm and exit building
- ☐ _____
- ☐ _____
- ☐ _____

Opening Procedure

Date _____

- ☐ Arrive at least 30 minutes before opening
- ☐ If there is any signs of forced entry, do not enter and call the police
- ☐ Never open store alone, two or more employees must be present with you
- ☐ Relock door after entering. Let employees in as they arrive
- ☐ Make a visual check of entire store to make sure nothing is out of place and everything looks clean
- ☐ Disable alarms
- ☐ Open safe, remove cash register tills, and set up cash registers
- ☐ Turn on computers at the front desk and make sure they're working properly
- ☐ Check e-mails and respond if needed
- ☐ Turn on display televisions and make sure the advertisements are properly broadcasting on loop
- ☐ Turn on game consoles and make sure they're working properly
- ☐ Organize displays in windows or around store floor
- ☐ Turn on AC/heater, adjust thermostat if needed
- ☐ Start daily task list
- ☐ Schedule lunch and breaks
- ☐ _____
- ☐ _____
- ☐ _____

Closing Procedure

Date _____

- ☐ Turn off any lights after all customers exit the building
- ☐ Turn off front lights
- ☐ Never leave store alone, always exit facility in pairs
- ☐ Place closed sign at window in plain sight
- ☐ Assign closing and cleaning duties to employees
- ☐ Make sure all bathrooms, shelves and floors are completely cleaned
- ☐ Return all refunded items behind front desk or in back room
- ☐ Return any refunded defected items to back room for processing
- ☐ Close out registers, make sure all funds are accounted for
- ☐ Settle credit card machines
- ☐ Generate a detailed batch listing
- ☐ Transmit batch
- ☐ Store all tills in safe and lock it
- ☐ Turn off AC/heat, computers, televisions and game consoles.
- ☐ Lock all necessary perimeter doors
- ☐ Set alarm and exit building
- ☐ _____
- ☐ _____
- ☐ _____

Opening Procedure

Date _____

- ☐ Arrive at least 30 minutes before opening
- ☐ If there is any signs of forced entry, do not enter and call the police
- ☐ Never open store alone, two or more employees must be present with you
- ☐ Relock door after entering. Let employees in as they arrive
- ☐ Make a visual check of entire store to make sure nothing is out of place and everything looks clean
- ☐ Disable alarms
- ☐ Open safe, remove cash register tills, and set up cash registers
- ☐ Turn on computers at the front desk and make sure they're working properly
- ☐ Check e-mails and respond if needed
- ☐ Turn on display televisions and make sure the advertisements are properly broadcasting on loop
- ☐ Turn on game consoles and make sure they're working properly
- ☐ Organize displays in windows or around store floor
- ☐ Turn on AC/heater, adjust thermostat if needed
- ☐ Start daily task list
- ☐ Schedule lunch and breaks
- ☐ _____
- ☐ _____
- ☐ _____

Closing Procedure

Date _____

- ❏ Turn off any lights after all customers exit the building
- ❏ Turn off front lights
- ❏ Never leave store alone, always exit facility in pairs
- ❏ Place closed sign at window in plain sight
- ❏ Assign closing and cleaning duties to employees
- ❏ Make sure all bathrooms, shelves and floors are completely cleaned
- ❏ Return all refunded items behind front desk or in back room
- ❏ Return any refunded defected items to back room for processing
- ❏ Close out registers, make sure all funds are accounted for
- ❏ Settle credit card machines
- ❏ Generate a detailed batch listing
- ❏ Transmit batch
- ❏ Store all tills in safe and lock it
- ❏ Turn off AC/heat, computers, televisions and game consoles.
- ❏ Lock all necessary perimeter doors
- ❏ Set alarm and exit building
- ❏ _____
- ❏ _____
- ❏ _____

Opening Procedure

Date _____

- ☐ Arrive at least 30 minutes before opening
- ☐ If there is any signs of forced entry, do not enter and call the police
- ☐ Never open store alone, two or more employees must be present with you
- ☐ Relock door after entering. Let employees in as they arrive
- ☐ Make a visual check of entire store to make sure nothing is out of place and everything looks clean
- ☐ Disable alarms
- ☐ Open safe, remove cash register tills, and set up cash registers
- ☐ Turn on computers at the front desk and make sure they're working properly
- ☐ Check e-mails and respond if needed
- ☐ Turn on display televisions and make sure the advertisements are properly broadcasting on loop
- ☐ Turn on game consoles and make sure they're working properly
- ☐ Organize displays in windows or around store floor
- ☐ Turn on AC/heater, adjust thermostat if needed
- ☐ Start daily task list
- ☐ Schedule lunch and breaks
- ☐ _____
- ☐ _____
- ☐ _____

Closing Procedure

Date _____

- ❑ Turn off any lights after all customers exit the building
- ❑ Turn off front lights
- ❑ Never leave store alone, always exit facility in pairs
- ❑ Place closed sign at window in plain sight
- ❑ Assign closing and cleaning duties to employees
- ❑ Make sure all bathrooms, shelves and floors are completely cleaned
- ❑ Return all refunded items behind front desk or in back room
- ❑ Return any refunded defected items to back room for processing
- ❑ Close out registers, make sure all funds are accounted for
- ❑ Settle credit card machines
- ❑ Generate a detailed batch listing
- ❑ Transmit batch
- ❑ Store all tills in safe and lock it
- ❑ Turn off AC/heat, computers, televisions and game consoles.
- ❑ Lock all necessary perimeter doors
- ❑ Set alarm and exit building
- ❑ _____
- ❑ _____
- ❑ _____

Opening Procedure

Date _____

- ☐ Arrive at least 30 minutes before opening
- ☐ If there is any signs of forced entry, do not enter and call the police
- ☐ Never open store alone, two or more employees must be present with you
- ☐ Relock door after entering. Let employees in as they arrive
- ☐ Make a visual check of entire store to make sure nothing is out of place and everything looks clean
- ☐ Disable alarms
- ☐ Open safe, remove cash register tills, and set up cash registers
- ☐ Turn on computers at the front desk and make sure they're working properly
- ☐ Check e-mails and respond if needed
- ☐ Turn on display televisions and make sure the advertisements are properly broadcasting on loop
- ☐ Turn on game consoles and make sure they're working properly
- ☐ Organize displays in windows or around store floor
- ☐ Turn on AC/heater, adjust thermostat if needed
- ☐ Start daily task list
- ☐ Schedule lunch and breaks
- ☐ _____
- ☐ _____
- ☐ _____

Closing Procedure

Date _____

- ☐ Turn off any lights after all customers exit the building
- ☐ Turn off front lights
- ☐ Never leave store alone, always exit facility in pairs
- ☐ Place closed sign at window in plain sight
- ☐ Assign closing and cleaning duties to employees
- ☐ Make sure all bathrooms, shelves and floors are completely cleaned
- ☐ Return all refunded items behind front desk or in back room
- ☐ Return any refunded defected items to back room for processing
- ☐ Close out registers, make sure all funds are accounted for
- ☐ Settle credit card machines
- ☐ Generate a detailed batch listing
- ☐ Transmit batch
- ☐ Store all tills in safe and lock it
- ☐ Turn off AC/heat, computers, televisions and game consoles.
- ☐ Lock all necessary perimeter doors
- ☐ Set alarm and exit building
- ☐ _____
- ☐ _____
- ☐ _____

Opening Procedure

Date _____

- ☐ Arrive at least 30 minutes before opening
- ☐ If there is any signs of forced entry, do not enter and call the police
- ☐ Never open store alone, two or more employees must be present with you
- ☐ Relock door after entering. Let employees in as they arrive
- ☐ Make a visual check of entire store to make sure nothing is out of place and everything looks clean
- ☐ Disable alarms
- ☐ Open safe, remove cash register tills, and set up cash registers
- ☐ Turn on computers at the front desk and make sure they're working properly
- ☐ Check e-mails and respond if needed
- ☐ Turn on display televisions and make sure the advertisements are properly broadcasting on loop
- ☐ Turn on game consoles and make sure they're working properly
- ☐ Organize displays in windows or around store floor
- ☐ Turn on AC/heater, adjust thermostat if needed
- ☐ Start daily task list
- ☐ Schedule lunch and breaks
- ☐ _____
- ☐ _____
- ☐ _____

Closing Procedure

Date _____

- ☐ Turn off any lights after all customers exit the building
- ☐ Turn off front lights
- ☐ Never leave store alone, always exit facility in pairs
- ☐ Place closed sign at window in plain sight
- ☐ Assign closing and cleaning duties to employees
- ☐ Make sure all bathrooms, shelves and floors are completely cleaned
- ☐ Return all refunded items behind front desk or in back room
- ☐ Return any refunded defected items to back room for processing
- ☐ Close out registers, make sure all funds are accounted for
- ☐ Settle credit card machines
- ☐ Generate a detailed batch listing
- ☐ Transmit batch
- ☐ Store all tills in safe and lock it
- ☐ Turn off AC/heat, computers, televisions and game consoles.
- ☐ Lock all necessary perimeter doors
- ☐ Set alarm and exit building
- ☐ _____
- ☐ _____
- ☐ _____

Opening Procedure

Date _____

- ☐ Arrive at least 30 minutes before opening
- ☐ If there is any signs of forced entry, do not enter and call the police
- ☐ Never open store alone, two or more employees must be present with you
- ☐ Relock door after entering. Let employees in as they arrive
- ☐ Make a visual check of entire store to make sure nothing is out of place and everything looks clean
- ☐ Disable alarms
- ☐ Open safe, remove cash register tills, and set up cash registers
- ☐ Turn on computers at the front desk and make sure they're working properly
- ☐ Check e-mails and respond if needed
- ☐ Turn on display televisions and make sure the advertisements are properly broadcasting on loop
- ☐ Turn on game consoles and make sure they're working properly
- ☐ Organize displays in windows or around store floor
- ☐ Turn on AC/heater, adjust thermostat if needed
- ☐ Start daily task list
- ☐ Schedule lunch and breaks
- ☐ _____
- ☐ _____
- ☐ _____

Closing Procedure

Date _____

- ☐ Turn off any lights after all customers exit the building
- ☐ Turn off front lights
- ☐ Never leave store alone, always exit facility in pairs
- ☐ Place closed sign at window in plain sight
- ☐ Assign closing and cleaning duties to employees
- ☐ Make sure all bathrooms, shelves and floors are completely cleaned
- ☐ Return all refunded items behind front desk or in back room
- ☐ Return any refunded defected items to back room for processing
- ☐ Close out registers, make sure all funds are accounted for
- ☐ Settle credit card machines
- ☐ Generate a detailed batch listing
- ☐ Transmit batch
- ☐ Store all tills in safe and lock it
- ☐ Turn off AC/heat, computers, televisions and game consoles.
- ☐ Lock all necessary perimeter doors
- ☐ Set alarm and exit building
- ☐ _____
- ☐ _____
- ☐ _____

Opening Procedure

Date _____

- ☐ Arrive at least 30 minutes before opening
- ☐ If there is any signs of forced entry, do not enter and call the police
- ☐ Never open store alone, two or more employees must be present with you
- ☐ Relock door after entering. Let employees in as they arrive
- ☐ Make a visual check of entire store to make sure nothing is out of place and everything looks clean
- ☐ Disable alarms
- ☐ Open safe, remove cash register tills, and set up cash registers
- ☐ Turn on computers at the front desk and make sure they're working properly
- ☐ Check e-mails and respond if needed
- ☐ Turn on display televisions and make sure the advertisements are properly broadcasting on loop
- ☐ Turn on game consoles and make sure they're working properly
- ☐ Organize displays in windows or around store floor
- ☐ Turn on AC/heater, adjust thermostat if needed
- ☐ Start daily task list
- ☐ Schedule lunch and breaks
- ☐ _____
- ☐ _____
- ☐ _____

Closing Procedure

Date _____

- ☐ Turn off any lights after all customers exit the building
- ☐ Turn off front lights
- ☐ Never leave store alone, always exit facility in pairs
- ☐ Place closed sign at window in plain sight
- ☐ Assign closing and cleaning duties to employees
- ☐ Make sure all bathrooms, shelves and floors are completely cleaned
- ☐ Return all refunded items behind front desk or in back room
- ☐ Return any refunded defected items to back room for processing
- ☐ Close out registers, make sure all funds are accounted for
- ☐ Settle credit card machines
- ☐ Generate a detailed batch listing
- ☐ Transmit batch
- ☐ Store all tills in safe and lock it
- ☐ Turn off AC/heat, computers, televisions and game consoles.
- ☐ Lock all necessary perimeter doors
- ☐ Set alarm and exit building
- ☐ _____
- ☐ _____
- ☐ _____

Opening Procedure

Date _____

- ❏ Arrive at least 30 minutes before opening
- ❏ If there is any signs of forced entry, do not enter and call the police
- ❏ Never open store alone, two or more employees must be present with you
- ❏ Relock door after entering. Let employees in as they arrive
- ❏ Make a visual check of entire store to make sure nothing is out of place and everything looks clean
- ❏ Disable alarms
- ❏ Open safe, remove cash register tills, and set up cash registers
- ❏ Turn on computers at the front desk and make sure they're working properly
- ❏ Check e-mails and respond if needed
- ❏ Turn on display televisions and make sure the advertisements are properly broadcasting on loop
- ❏ Turn on game consoles and make sure they're working properly
- ❏ Organize displays in windows or around store floor
- ❏ Turn on AC/heater, adjust thermostat if needed
- ❏ Start daily task list
- ❏ Schedule lunch and breaks
- ❏ _____
- ❏ _____
- ❏ _____

Closing Procedure

Date _____

- ☐ Turn off any lights after all customers exit the building
- ☐ Turn off front lights
- ☐ Never leave store alone, always exit facility in pairs
- ☐ Place closed sign at window in plain sight
- ☐ Assign closing and cleaning duties to employees
- ☐ Make sure all bathrooms, shelves and floors are completely cleaned
- ☐ Return all refunded items behind front desk or in back room
- ☐ Return any refunded defected items to back room for processing
- ☐ Close out registers, make sure all funds are accounted for
- ☐ Settle credit card machines
- ☐ Generate a detailed batch listing
- ☐ Transmit batch
- ☐ Store all tills in safe and lock it
- ☐ Turn off AC/heat, computers, televisions and game consoles.
- ☐ Lock all necessary perimeter doors
- ☐ Set alarm and exit building
- ☐ _____
- ☐ _____
- ☐ _____

Opening Procedure

Date _____

- ❑ Arrive at least 30 minutes before opening
- ❑ If there is any signs of forced entry, do not enter and call the police
- ❑ Never open store alone, two or more employees must be present with you
- ❑ Relock door after entering. Let employees in as they arrive
- ❑ Make a visual check of entire store to make sure nothing is out of place and everything looks clean
- ❑ Disable alarms
- ❑ Open safe, remove cash register tills, and set up cash registers
- ❑ Turn on computers at the front desk and make sure they're working properly
- ❑ Check e-mails and respond if needed
- ❑ Turn on display televisions and make sure the advertisements are properly broadcasting on loop
- ❑ Turn on game consoles and make sure they're working properly
- ❑ Organize displays in windows or around store floor
- ❑ Turn on AC/heater, adjust thermostat if needed
- ❑ Start daily task list
- ❑ Schedule lunch and breaks
- ❑ _____
- ❑ _____
- ❑ _____

Closing Procedure

Date _____

- ☐ Turn off any lights after all customers exit the building
- ☐ Turn off front lights
- ☐ Never leave store alone, always exit facility in pairs
- ☐ Place closed sign at window in plain sight
- ☐ Assign closing and cleaning duties to employees
- ☐ Make sure all bathrooms, shelves and floors are completely cleaned
- ☐ Return all refunded items behind front desk or in back room
- ☐ Return any refunded defected items to back room for processing
- ☐ Close out registers, make sure all funds are accounted for
- ☐ Settle credit card machines
- ☐ Generate a detailed batch listing
- ☐ Transmit batch
- ☐ Store all tills in safe and lock it
- ☐ Turn off AC/heat, computers, televisions and game consoles.
- ☐ Lock all necessary perimeter doors
- ☐ Set alarm and exit building
- ☐ _____
- ☐ _____
- ☐ _____

Opening Procedure

Date _____

- ❏ Arrive at least 30 minutes before opening
- ❏ If there is any signs of forced entry, do not enter and call the police
- ❏ Never open store alone, two or more employees must be present with you
- ❏ Relock door after entering. Let employees in as they arrive
- ❏ Make a visual check of entire store to make sure nothing is out of place and everything looks clean
- ❏ Disable alarms
- ❏ Open safe, remove cash register tills, and set up cash registers
- ❏ Turn on computers at the front desk and make sure they're working properly
- ❏ Check e-mails and respond if needed
- ❏ Turn on display televisions and make sure the advertisements are properly broadcasting on loop
- ❏ Turn on game consoles and make sure they're working properly
- ❏ Organize displays in windows or around store floor
- ❏ Turn on AC/heater, adjust thermostat if needed
- ❏ Start daily task list
- ❏ Schedule lunch and breaks
- ❏ _____
- ❏ _____
- ❏ _____

Closing Procedure

Date _____

- ☐ Turn off any lights after all customers exit the building
- ☐ Turn off front lights
- ☐ Never leave store alone, always exit facility in pairs
- ☐ Place closed sign at window in plain sight
- ☐ Assign closing and cleaning duties to employees
- ☐ Make sure all bathrooms, shelves and floors are completely cleaned
- ☐ Return all refunded items behind front desk or in back room
- ☐ Return any refunded defected items to back room for processing
- ☐ Close out registers, make sure all funds are accounted for
- ☐ Settle credit card machines
- ☐ Generate a detailed batch listing
- ☐ Transmit batch
- ☐ Store all tills in safe and lock it
- ☐ Turn off AC/heat, computers, televisions and game consoles.
- ☐ Lock all necessary perimeter doors
- ☐ Set alarm and exit building
- ☐ _____
- ☐ _____
- ☐ _____

Opening Procedure

Date _____

- ❏ Arrive at least 30 minutes before opening
- ❏ If there is any signs of forced entry, do not enter and call the police
- ❏ Never open store alone, two or more employees must be present with you
- ❏ Relock door after entering. Let employees in as they arrive
- ❏ Make a visual check of entire store to make sure nothing is out of place and everything looks clean
- ❏ Disable alarms
- ❏ Open safe, remove cash register tills, and set up cash registers
- ❏ Turn on computers at the front desk and make sure they're working properly
- ❏ Check e-mails and respond if needed
- ❏ Turn on display televisions and make sure the advertisements are properly broadcasting on loop
- ❏ Turn on game consoles and make sure they're working properly
- ❏ Organize displays in windows or around store floor
- ❏ Turn on AC/heater, adjust thermostat if needed
- ❏ Start daily task list
- ❏ Schedule lunch and breaks
- ❏ _____
- ❏ _____
- ❏ _____

Closing Procedure

Date _____

- ☐ Turn off any lights after all customers exit the building
- ☐ Turn off front lights
- ☐ Never leave store alone, always exit facility in pairs
- ☐ Place closed sign at window in plain sight
- ☐ Assign closing and cleaning duties to employees
- ☐ Make sure all bathrooms, shelves and floors are completely cleaned
- ☐ Return all refunded items behind front desk or in back room
- ☐ Return any refunded defected items to back room for processing
- ☐ Close out registers, make sure all funds are accounted for
- ☐ Settle credit card machines
- ☐ Generate a detailed batch listing
- ☐ Transmit batch
- ☐ Store all tills in safe and lock it
- ☐ Turn off AC/heat, computers, televisions and game consoles.
- ☐ Lock all necessary perimeter doors
- ☐ Set alarm and exit building
- ☐ _____
- ☐ _____
- ☐ _____

Opening Procedure

Date _____

- ☐ Arrive at least 30 minutes before opening
- ☐ If there is any signs of forced entry, do not enter and call the police
- ☐ Never open store alone, two or more employees must be present with you
- ☐ Relock door after entering. Let employees in as they arrive
- ☐ Make a visual check of entire store to make sure nothing is out of place and everything looks clean
- ☐ Disable alarms
- ☐ Open safe, remove cash register tills, and set up cash registers
- ☐ Turn on computers at the front desk and make sure they're working properly
- ☐ Check e-mails and respond if needed
- ☐ Turn on display televisions and make sure the advertisements are properly broadcasting on loop
- ☐ Turn on game consoles and make sure they're working properly
- ☐ Organize displays in windows or around store floor
- ☐ Turn on AC/heater, adjust thermostat if needed
- ☐ Start daily task list
- ☐ Schedule lunch and breaks
- ☐ _____
- ☐ _____
- ☐ _____

Closing Procedure

Date _____

- ☐ Turn off any lights after all customers exit the building
- ☐ Turn off front lights
- ☐ Never leave store alone, always exit facility in pairs
- ☐ Place closed sign at window in plain sight
- ☐ Assign closing and cleaning duties to employees
- ☐ Make sure all bathrooms, shelves and floors are completely cleaned
- ☐ Return all refunded items behind front desk or in back room
- ☐ Return any refunded defected items to back room for processing
- ☐ Close out registers, make sure all funds are accounted for
- ☐ Settle credit card machines
- ☐ Generate a detailed batch listing
- ☐ Transmit batch
- ☐ Store all tills in safe and lock it
- ☐ Turn off AC/heat, computers, televisions and game consoles.
- ☐ Lock all necessary perimeter doors
- ☐ Set alarm and exit building
- ☐ _____
- ☐ _____
- ☐ _____

Opening Procedure

Date _____

- ☐ Arrive at least 30 minutes before opening
- ☐ If there is any signs of forced entry, do not enter and call the police
- ☐ Never open store alone, two or more employees must be present with you
- ☐ Relock door after entering. Let employees in as they arrive
- ☐ Make a visual check of entire store to make sure nothing is out of place and everything looks clean
- ☐ Disable alarms
- ☐ Open safe, remove cash register tills, and set up cash registers
- ☐ Turn on computers at the front desk and make sure they're working properly
- ☐ Check e-mails and respond if needed
- ☐ Turn on display televisions and make sure the advertisements are properly broadcasting on loop
- ☐ Turn on game consoles and make sure they're working properly
- ☐ Organize displays in windows or around store floor
- ☐ Turn on AC/heater, adjust thermostat if needed
- ☐ Start daily task list
- ☐ Schedule lunch and breaks
- ☐ _____
- ☐ _____
- ☐ _____

Closing Procedure

Date _____

- ☐ Turn off any lights after all customers exit the building
- ☐ Turn off front lights
- ☐ Never leave store alone, always exit facility in pairs
- ☐ Place closed sign at window in plain sight
- ☐ Assign closing and cleaning duties to employees
- ☐ Make sure all bathrooms, shelves and floors are completely cleaned
- ☐ Return all refunded items behind front desk or in back room
- ☐ Return any refunded defected items to back room for processing
- ☐ Close out registers, make sure all funds are accounted for
- ☐ Settle credit card machines
- ☐ Generate a detailed batch listing
- ☐ Transmit batch
- ☐ Store all tills in safe and lock it
- ☐ Turn off AC/heat, computers, televisions and game consoles.
- ☐ Lock all necessary perimeter doors
- ☐ Set alarm and exit building
- ☐ _____
- ☐ _____
- ☐ _____

Opening Procedure

Date _____

- ☐ Arrive at least 30 minutes before opening
- ☐ If there is any signs of forced entry, do not enter and call the police
- ☐ Never open store alone, two or more employees must be present with you
- ☐ Relock door after entering. Let employees in as they arrive
- ☐ Make a visual check of entire store to make sure nothing is out of place and everything looks clean
- ☐ Disable alarms
- ☐ Open safe, remove cash register tills, and set up cash registers
- ☐ Turn on computers at the front desk and make sure they're working properly
- ☐ Check e-mails and respond if needed
- ☐ Turn on display televisions and make sure the advertisements are properly broadcasting on loop
- ☐ Turn on game consoles and make sure they're working properly
- ☐ Organize displays in windows or around store floor
- ☐ Turn on AC/heater, adjust thermostat if needed
- ☐ Start daily task list
- ☐ Schedule lunch and breaks
- ☐ _____
- ☐ _____
- ☐ _____

Closing Procedure

Date _____

- ☐ Turn off any lights after all customers exit the building
- ☐ Turn off front lights
- ☐ Never leave store alone, always exit facility in pairs
- ☐ Place closed sign at window in plain sight
- ☐ Assign closing and cleaning duties to employees
- ☐ Make sure all bathrooms, shelves and floors are completely cleaned
- ☐ Return all refunded items behind front desk or in back room
- ☐ Return any refunded defected items to back room for processing
- ☐ Close out registers, make sure all funds are accounted for
- ☐ Settle credit card machines
- ☐ Generate a detailed batch listing
- ☐ Transmit batch
- ☐ Store all tills in safe and lock it
- ☐ Turn off AC/heat, computers, televisions and game consoles.
- ☐ Lock all necessary perimeter doors
- ☐ Set alarm and exit building
- ☐ _____
- ☐ _____
- ☐ _____

Opening Procedure

Date _____

- ❑ Arrive at least 30 minutes before opening
- ❑ If there is any signs of forced entry, do not enter and call the police
- ❑ Never open store alone, two or more employees must be present with you
- ❑ Relock door after entering. Let employees in as they arrive
- ❑ Make a visual check of entire store to make sure nothing is out of place and everything looks clean
- ❑ Disable alarms
- ❑ Open safe, remove cash register tills, and set up cash registers
- ❑ Turn on computers at the front desk and make sure they're working properly
- ❑ Check e-mails and respond if needed
- ❑ Turn on display televisions and make sure the advertisements are properly broadcasting on loop
- ❑ Turn on game consoles and make sure they're working properly
- ❑ Organize displays in windows or around store floor
- ❑ Turn on AC/heater, adjust thermostat if needed
- ❑ Start daily task list
- ❑ Schedule lunch and breaks
- ❑ _____
- ❑ _____
- ❑ _____

Closing Procedure

Date _____

- ☐ Turn off any lights after all customers exit the building
- ☐ Turn off front lights
- ☐ Never leave store alone, always exit facility in pairs
- ☐ Place closed sign at window in plain sight
- ☐ Assign closing and cleaning duties to employees
- ☐ Make sure all bathrooms, shelves and floors are completely cleaned
- ☐ Return all refunded items behind front desk or in back room
- ☐ Return any refunded defected items to back room for processing
- ☐ Close out registers, make sure all funds are accounted for
- ☐ Settle credit card machines
- ☐ Generate a detailed batch listing
- ☐ Transmit batch
- ☐ Store all tills in safe and lock it
- ☐ Turn off AC/heat, computers, televisions and game consoles.
- ☐ Lock all necessary perimeter doors
- ☐ Set alarm and exit building
- ☐ _____
- ☐ _____
- ☐ _____

Opening Procedure

Date _____

- ☐ Arrive at least 30 minutes before opening
- ☐ If there is any signs of forced entry, do not enter and call the police
- ☐ Never open store alone, two or more employees must be present with you
- ☐ Relock door after entering. Let employees in as they arrive
- ☐ Make a visual check of entire store to make sure nothing is out of place and everything looks clean
- ☐ Disable alarms
- ☐ Open safe, remove cash register tills, and set up cash registers
- ☐ Turn on computers at the front desk and make sure they're working properly
- ☐ Check e-mails and respond if needed
- ☐ Turn on display televisions and make sure the advertisements are properly broadcasting on loop
- ☐ Turn on game consoles and make sure they're working properly
- ☐ Organize displays in windows or around store floor
- ☐ Turn on AC/heater, adjust thermostat if needed
- ☐ Start daily task list
- ☐ Schedule lunch and breaks
- ☐ _____
- ☐ _____
- ☐ _____

Closing Procedure

Date _____

- ☐ Turn off any lights after all customers exit the building
- ☐ Turn off front lights
- ☐ Never leave store alone, always exit facility in pairs
- ☐ Place closed sign at window in plain sight
- ☐ Assign closing and cleaning duties to employees
- ☐ Make sure all bathrooms, shelves and floors are completely cleaned
- ☐ Return all refunded items behind front desk or in back room
- ☐ Return any refunded defected items to back room for processing
- ☐ Close out registers, make sure all funds are accounted for
- ☐ Settle credit card machines
- ☐ Generate a detailed batch listing
- ☐ Transmit batch
- ☐ Store all tills in safe and lock it
- ☐ Turn off AC/heat, computers, televisions and game consoles.
- ☐ Lock all necessary perimeter doors
- ☐ Set alarm and exit building
- ☐ _____
- ☐ _____
- ☐ _____

Opening Procedure

Date _____

- ☐ Arrive at least 30 minutes before opening
- ☐ If there is any signs of forced entry, do not enter and call the police
- ☐ Never open store alone, two or more employees must be present with you
- ☐ Relock door after entering. Let employees in as they arrive
- ☐ Make a visual check of entire store to make sure nothing is out of place and everything looks clean
- ☐ Disable alarms
- ☐ Open safe, remove cash register tills, and set up cash registers
- ☐ Turn on computers at the front desk and make sure they're working properly
- ☐ Check e-mails and respond if needed
- ☐ Turn on display televisions and make sure the advertisements are properly broadcasting on loop
- ☐ Turn on game consoles and make sure they're working properly
- ☐ Organize displays in windows or around store floor
- ☐ Turn on AC/heater, adjust thermostat if needed
- ☐ Start daily task list
- ☐ Schedule lunch and breaks
- ☐ _____
- ☐ _____
- ☐ _____

Closing Procedure

Date _____

- ☐ Turn off any lights after all customers exit the building
- ☐ Turn off front lights
- ☐ Never leave store alone, always exit facility in pairs
- ☐ Place closed sign at window in plain sight
- ☐ Assign closing and cleaning duties to employees
- ☐ Make sure all bathrooms, shelves and floors are completely cleaned
- ☐ Return all refunded items behind front desk or in back room
- ☐ Return any refunded defected items to back room for processing
- ☐ Close out registers, make sure all funds are accounted for
- ☐ Settle credit card machines
- ☐ Generate a detailed batch listing
- ☐ Transmit batch
- ☐ Store all tills in safe and lock it
- ☐ Turn off AC/heat, computers, televisions and game consoles.
- ☐ Lock all necessary perimeter doors
- ☐ Set alarm and exit building
- ☐ _____
- ☐ _____
- ☐ _____

Opening Procedure

Date _____

- ☐ Arrive at least 30 minutes before opening
- ☐ If there is any signs of forced entry, do not enter and call the police
- ☐ Never open store alone, two or more employees must be present with you
- ☐ Relock door after entering. Let employees in as they arrive
- ☐ Make a visual check of entire store to make sure nothing is out of place and everything looks clean
- ☐ Disable alarms
- ☐ Open safe, remove cash register tills, and set up cash registers
- ☐ Turn on computers at the front desk and make sure they're working properly
- ☐ Check e-mails and respond if needed
- ☐ Turn on display televisions and make sure the advertisements are properly broadcasting on loop
- ☐ Turn on game consoles and make sure they're working properly
- ☐ Organize displays in windows or around store floor
- ☐ Turn on AC/heater, adjust thermostat if needed
- ☐ Start daily task list
- ☐ Schedule lunch and breaks
- ☐ _____
- ☐ _____
- ☐ _____

Closing Procedure

Date _____

- ☐ Turn off any lights after all customers exit the building
- ☐ Turn off front lights
- ☐ Never leave store alone, always exit facility in pairs
- ☐ Place closed sign at window in plain sight
- ☐ Assign closing and cleaning duties to employees
- ☐ Make sure all bathrooms, shelves and floors are completely cleaned
- ☐ Return all refunded items behind front desk or in back room
- ☐ Return any refunded defected items to back room for processing
- ☐ Close out registers, make sure all funds are accounted for
- ☐ Settle credit card machines
- ☐ Generate a detailed batch listing
- ☐ Transmit batch
- ☐ Store all tills in safe and lock it
- ☐ Turn off AC/heat, computers, televisions and game consoles.
- ☐ Lock all necessary perimeter doors
- ☐ Set alarm and exit building
- ☐ _____
- ☐ _____
- ☐ _____

Opening Procedure

Date _____

- ☐ Arrive at least 30 minutes before opening
- ☐ If there is any signs of forced entry, do not enter and call the police
- ☐ Never open store alone, two or more employees must be present with you
- ☐ Relock door after entering. Let employees in as they arrive
- ☐ Make a visual check of entire store to make sure nothing is out of place and everything looks clean
- ☐ Disable alarms
- ☐ Open safe, remove cash register tills, and set up cash registers
- ☐ Turn on computers at the front desk and make sure they're working properly
- ☐ Check e-mails and respond if needed
- ☐ Turn on display televisions and make sure the advertisements are properly broadcasting on loop
- ☐ Turn on game consoles and make sure they're working properly
- ☐ Organize displays in windows or around store floor
- ☐ Turn on AC/heater, adjust thermostat if needed
- ☐ Start daily task list
- ☐ Schedule lunch and breaks
- ☐ _____
- ☐ _____
- ☐ _____

Closing Procedure

Date _____

- ☐ Turn off any lights after all customers exit the building
- ☐ Turn off front lights
- ☐ Never leave store alone, always exit facility in pairs
- ☐ Place closed sign at window in plain sight
- ☐ Assign closing and cleaning duties to employees
- ☐ Make sure all bathrooms, shelves and floors are completely cleaned
- ☐ Return all refunded items behind front desk or in back room
- ☐ Return any refunded defected items to back room for processing
- ☐ Close out registers, make sure all funds are accounted for
- ☐ Settle credit card machines
- ☐ Generate a detailed batch listing
- ☐ Transmit batch
- ☐ Store all tills in safe and lock it
- ☐ Turn off AC/heat, computers, televisions and game consoles.
- ☐ Lock all necessary perimeter doors
- ☐ Set alarm and exit building
- ☐ _____
- ☐ _____
- ☐ _____

Opening Procedure

Date _____

- ☐ Arrive at least 30 minutes before opening
- ☐ If there is any signs of forced entry, do not enter and call the police
- ☐ Never open store alone, two or more employees must be present with you
- ☐ Relock door after entering. Let employees in as they arrive
- ☐ Make a visual check of entire store to make sure nothing is out of place and everything looks clean
- ☐ Disable alarms
- ☐ Open safe, remove cash register tills, and set up cash registers
- ☐ Turn on computers at the front desk and make sure they're working properly
- ☐ Check e-mails and respond if needed
- ☐ Turn on display televisions and make sure the advertisements are properly broadcasting on loop
- ☐ Turn on game consoles and make sure they're working properly
- ☐ Organize displays in windows or around store floor
- ☐ Turn on AC/heater, adjust thermostat if needed
- ☐ Start daily task list
- ☐ Schedule lunch and breaks
- ☐ _____
- ☐ _____
- ☐ _____

Closing Procedure

Date _____

- ❑ Turn off any lights after all customers exit the building
- ❑ Turn off front lights
- ❑ Never leave store alone, always exit facility in pairs
- ❑ Place closed sign at window in plain sight
- ❑ Assign closing and cleaning duties to employees
- ❑ Make sure all bathrooms, shelves and floors are completely cleaned
- ❑ Return all refunded items behind front desk or in back room
- ❑ Return any refunded defected items to back room for processing
- ❑ Close out registers, make sure all funds are accounted for
- ❑ Settle credit card machines
- ❑ Generate a detailed batch listing
- ❑ Transmit batch
- ❑ Store all tills in safe and lock it
- ❑ Turn off AC/heat, computers, televisions and game consoles.
- ❑ Lock all necessary perimeter doors
- ❑ Set alarm and exit building
- ❑ _____
- ❑ _____
- ❑ _____

Opening Procedure

Date _____

- ❏ Arrive at least 30 minutes before opening
- ❏ If there is any signs of forced entry, do not enter and call the police
- ❏ Never open store alone, two or more employees must be present with you
- ❏ Relock door after entering. Let employees in as they arrive
- ❏ Make a visual check of entire store to make sure nothing is out of place and everything looks clean
- ❏ Disable alarms
- ❏ Open safe, remove cash register tills, and set up cash registers
- ❏ Turn on computers at the front desk and make sure they're working properly
- ❏ Check e-mails and respond if needed
- ❏ Turn on display televisions and make sure the advertisements are properly broadcasting on loop
- ❏ Turn on game consoles and make sure they're working properly
- ❏ Organize displays in windows or around store floor
- ❏ Turn on AC/heater, adjust thermostat if needed
- ❏ Start daily task list
- ❏ Schedule lunch and breaks
- ❏ _____
- ❏ _____
- ❏ _____

Closing Procedure

Date _____

- ❑ Turn off any lights after all customers exit the building
- ❑ Turn off front lights
- ❑ Never leave store alone, always exit facility in pairs
- ❑ Place closed sign at window in plain sight
- ❑ Assign closing and cleaning duties to employees
- ❑ Make sure all bathrooms, shelves and floors are completely cleaned
- ❑ Return all refunded items behind front desk or in back room
- ❑ Return any refunded defected items to back room for processing
- ❑ Close out registers, make sure all funds are accounted for
- ❑ Settle credit card machines
- ❑ Generate a detailed batch listing
- ❑ Transmit batch
- ❑ Store all tills in safe and lock it
- ❑ Turn off AC/heat, computers, televisions and game consoles.
- ❑ Lock all necessary perimeter doors
- ❑ Set alarm and exit building
- ❑ _____
- ❑ _____
- ❑ _____

Opening Procedure

Date _____

- ☐ Arrive at least 30 minutes before opening
- ☐ If there is any signs of forced entry, do not enter and call the police
- ☐ Never open store alone, two or more employees must be present with you
- ☐ Relock door after entering. Let employees in as they arrive
- ☐ Make a visual check of entire store to make sure nothing is out of place and everything looks clean
- ☐ Disable alarms
- ☐ Open safe, remove cash register tills, and set up cash registers
- ☐ Turn on computers at the front desk and make sure they're working properly
- ☐ Check e-mails and respond if needed
- ☐ Turn on display televisions and make sure the advertisements are properly broadcasting on loop
- ☐ Turn on game consoles and make sure they're working properly
- ☐ Organize displays in windows or around store floor
- ☐ Turn on AC/heater, adjust thermostat if needed
- ☐ Start daily task list
- ☐ Schedule lunch and breaks
- ☐ _____
- ☐ _____
- ☐ _____

Closing Procedure

Date _____

- ☐ Turn off any lights after all customers exit the building
- ☐ Turn off front lights
- ☐ Never leave store alone, always exit facility in pairs
- ☐ Place closed sign at window in plain sight
- ☐ Assign closing and cleaning duties to employees
- ☐ Make sure all bathrooms, shelves and floors are completely cleaned
- ☐ Return all refunded items behind front desk or in back room
- ☐ Return any refunded defected items to back room for processing
- ☐ Close out registers, make sure all funds are accounted for
- ☐ Settle credit card machines
- ☐ Generate a detailed batch listing
- ☐ Transmit batch
- ☐ Store all tills in safe and lock it
- ☐ Turn off AC/heat, computers, televisions and game consoles.
- ☐ Lock all necessary perimeter doors
- ☐ Set alarm and exit building
- ☐ _____
- ☐ _____
- ☐ _____

Opening Procedure

Date _____

- ☐ Arrive at least 30 minutes before opening
- ☐ If there is any signs of forced entry, do not enter and call the police
- ☐ Never open store alone, two or more employees must be present with you
- ☐ Relock door after entering. Let employees in as they arrive
- ☐ Make a visual check of entire store to make sure nothing is out of place and everything looks clean
- ☐ Disable alarms
- ☐ Open safe, remove cash register tills, and set up cash registers
- ☐ Turn on computers at the front desk and make sure they're working properly
- ☐ Check e-mails and respond if needed
- ☐ Turn on display televisions and make sure the advertisements are properly broadcasting on loop
- ☐ Turn on game consoles and make sure they're working properly
- ☐ Organize displays in windows or around store floor
- ☐ Turn on AC/heater, adjust thermostat if needed
- ☐ Start daily task list
- ☐ Schedule lunch and breaks
- ☐ _____
- ☐ _____
- ☐ _____

Closing Procedure

Date _____

- ☐ Turn off any lights after all customers exit the building
- ☐ Turn off front lights
- ☐ Never leave store alone, always exit facility in pairs
- ☐ Place closed sign at window in plain sight
- ☐ Assign closing and cleaning duties to employees
- ☐ Make sure all bathrooms, shelves and floors are completely cleaned
- ☐ Return all refunded items behind front desk or in back room
- ☐ Return any refunded defected items to back room for processing
- ☐ Close out registers, make sure all funds are accounted for
- ☐ Settle credit card machines
- ☐ Generate a detailed batch listing
- ☐ Transmit batch
- ☐ Store all tills in safe and lock it
- ☐ Turn off AC/heat, computers, televisions and game consoles.
- ☐ Lock all necessary perimeter doors
- ☐ Set alarm and exit building
- ☐ _____
- ☐ _____
- ☐ _____

Opening Procedure

Date _____

- ☐ Arrive at least 30 minutes before opening
- ☐ If there is any signs of forced entry, do not enter and call the police
- ☐ Never open store alone, two or more employees must be present with you
- ☐ Relock door after entering. Let employees in as they arrive
- ☐ Make a visual check of entire store to make sure nothing is out of place and everything looks clean
- ☐ Disable alarms
- ☐ Open safe, remove cash register tills, and set up cash registers
- ☐ Turn on computers at the front desk and make sure they're working properly
- ☐ Check e-mails and respond if needed
- ☐ Turn on display televisions and make sure the advertisements are properly broadcasting on loop
- ☐ Turn on game consoles and make sure they're working properly
- ☐ Organize displays in windows or around store floor
- ☐ Turn on AC/heater, adjust thermostat if needed
- ☐ Start daily task list
- ☐ Schedule lunch and breaks
- ☐ _____
- ☐ _____
- ☐ _____

Closing Procedure

Date _____

- ☐ Turn off any lights after all customers exit the building
- ☐ Turn off front lights
- ☐ Never leave store alone, always exit facility in pairs
- ☐ Place closed sign at window in plain sight
- ☐ Assign closing and cleaning duties to employees
- ☐ Make sure all bathrooms, shelves and floors are completely cleaned
- ☐ Return all refunded items behind front desk or in back room
- ☐ Return any refunded defected items to back room for processing
- ☐ Close out registers, make sure all funds are accounted for
- ☐ Settle credit card machines
- ☐ Generate a detailed batch listing
- ☐ Transmit batch
- ☐ Store all tills in safe and lock it
- ☐ Turn off AC/heat, computers, televisions and game consoles.
- ☐ Lock all necessary perimeter doors
- ☐ Set alarm and exit building
- ☐ _____
- ☐ _____
- ☐ _____

Opening Procedure

Date _____

- ☐ Arrive at least 30 minutes before opening
- ☐ If there is any signs of forced entry, do not enter and call the police
- ☐ Never open store alone, two or more employees must be present with you
- ☐ Relock door after entering. Let employees in as they arrive
- ☐ Make a visual check of entire store to make sure nothing is out of place and everything looks clean
- ☐ Disable alarms
- ☐ Open safe, remove cash register tills, and set up cash registers
- ☐ Turn on computers at the front desk and make sure they're working properly
- ☐ Check e-mails and respond if needed
- ☐ Turn on display televisions and make sure the advertisements are properly broadcasting on loop
- ☐ Turn on game consoles and make sure they're working properly
- ☐ Organize displays in windows or around store floor
- ☐ Turn on AC/heater, adjust thermostat if needed
- ☐ Start daily task list
- ☐ Schedule lunch and breaks
- ☐ _____
- ☐ _____
- ☐ _____

Closing Procedure

Date _____

- ☐ Turn off any lights after all customers exit the building
- ☐ Turn off front lights
- ☐ Never leave store alone, always exit facility in pairs
- ☐ Place closed sign at window in plain sight
- ☐ Assign closing and cleaning duties to employees
- ☐ Make sure all bathrooms, shelves and floors are completely cleaned
- ☐ Return all refunded items behind front desk or in back room
- ☐ Return any refunded defected items to back room for processing
- ☐ Close out registers, make sure all funds are accounted for
- ☐ Settle credit card machines
- ☐ Generate a detailed batch listing
- ☐ Transmit batch
- ☐ Store all tills in safe and lock it
- ☐ Turn off AC/heat, computers, televisions and game consoles.
- ☐ Lock all necessary perimeter doors
- ☐ Set alarm and exit building
- ☐ _____
- ☐ _____
- ☐ _____

Thank you for your purchase of this workbook. We hope it helps you in your day-to-day procedures.

www.ingramcontent.com/pod-product-compliance
Lightning Source LLC
Chambersburg PA
CBHW070227210526
45169CB00023B/1012